A RETURN TO SIMPLER LIVING

EARLY AMERICAN COUNTRY HOMES

A RETURN TO SIMPLER LIVING

EARLY AMERICAN COUNTRY HOMES

TIM TANNER

GIBBS SMITH
TO ENRICH AND INSPIRE HUMANKIND

To Dad, Mom, and an innumerable list of Ancestors—who left me a rich heritage;
To Johnna, McKeand, Molly, and Noah—who support me in my pursuit of dreams;
and to my Progeny—reflect often on your noble origins.

". . . And he shall turn the heart of the fathers to the children,
and the heart of the children to their fathers . . ."
—Malachi 4:6

First Edition
15 14 13 12   5 4 3 2

Published by
Gibbs Smith
P.O. Box 667
Layton, Utah 84041
1.800.835.4993 orders
www.gibbs-smith.com

Photographs by Tim Tanner, Brian Brown, and Johnna Tanner
Cover and Book Design by Michelle Farinella Design

Gibbs Smith books are printed on paper produced from sustainable PEFC-certified forest/controlled wood source. Learn more at www.pefc.org.

Printed and bound in Hong Kong

Library of Congress Cataloging-in-Publication Data

Tanner, Tim.
  Early American country homes : a return to simpler living / Tim Tanner. — 1st ed.
    p. cm.
  ISBN 978-1-4236-2093-8 (alk. paper)
1. Antiques in interior decoration—United States. 2. Decoration and ornament, Rustic—United States. I. Title. II. Title: Return to simpler living.
  NK2115.5.A5T36 2011
  747.0973—dc22
                    2011013853

Acknowledgments

It is said that it takes a community to raise a child. 'Tis certainly the case to create a book, as well.

First of all, my thanks go to Gibbs Smith, for allowing me this opportunity, and to editors Bob Cooper and Madge Baird, for taking my proverbial sow's ear of literary skills and bringing them closer to the vicinity of a silk purse.

Johnna, my wife, deserves the Superhuman Award for her support, patience, and contributions.

Immeasurable gratitude goes to David T. Smith, Noah H. Bradley III, and Denny Walker, who so helpfully directed me to many of the homes in this book. Words cannot express my admiration and appreciation for not only their work, but for their warm personalities as well.

Brian Brown is the recipient of a mountain of my sincerest thanks. The best photographs in this book are undoubtedly his—and if I took a few good ones, the credit goes to his abilities as a teacher. I'm also appreciative of the folks at Old Sturbridge Village and the LDS Church historic sites for their kindness in letting us photograph at those wonderful locations.

Last—and far from least—a huge, warm thank you to the owners of each of the following homes. I have loved seeing your dwelling places, and treasure you as newfound friends. Thank you so much!

Tim Tanner

Table *of* Contents

Introduction

Home. This one word alone conjures up countless images, thoughts, and emotions. It is said that a picture is worth a thousand words, but some words in the English language say so much more than just a simple definition—like the word "home." In this case, the word invokes a thousand pictures, and although the images are slightly different for each of us, all of them are personal, warm, and comfortably cozy. Not only do we envision images from the recesses of our minds, but sounds, smells, even feelings begin parading across the stage of our consciousness. A warm, crackling fire in the hearth; a soft, overstuffed chair; Grandpa raking crimson and golden leaves in the crisp autumn air; pumpkins, corn stalks, and hot cider; pancakes smothered in warm maple syrup; a knowing smile on the face of a loved one. Home is something down deep inside each of us, tucked into a very special place.

Our current modern world is not exactly "cozy." Oh, there are aspects of our modern living that are especially praiseworthy—hot showers, indoor plumbing, automatic dishwashers. My bet is that if our ancestors could trade places with us, most would jump at the chance. But our modern world comes with its own set of challenges. Many twenty-first–century inventions have been developed to save us time and simplify our lives. Cell phones, Wi-Fi Internet service, cars that automatically lock the doors for us . . . the list goes on and on. I don't know about you, but my life doesn't seem simplified by the technological advances. In fact, although I'm happy to have it, all of the technology often makes me yearn even more for simplicity. How many modern homes ironically display those little (or big) countrified signs that read "Simplify"?

When it comes to pointing out the drawbacks of technology, I am perhaps the last person who should be calling the kettle black, sitting here typing on my iMac and processing digital photos for this book. But I often ask myself, "Why is it that I am so drawn to simple, historical buildings, furnishings, and styles—and why am I not alone?" Antiques have long had an appeal to some eyes (at least in the last 100 years or so), but beauty is in the eye of the beholder, right? So why do some of us go gaga over an old, beat-up, half-broken, paint-worn, unsophisticated cabinet, chair, or box?

"Could Someone Please Stop the Train?"

Somewhere deep down inside of us, we all yearn for peace—simple, quiet, calm peace. If we look in a dictionary, we won't find the word "home" as a synonym for "peace," but in our inner consciousness, those words all belong together: simple, calm, home, peace, quiet.

Could our modern innovations make us long even more for peace, quiet, and home? Could the contrast of our modern, hectic world make peaceful surroundings even more desirable? I recently completed the building of a very simple, spare, primitive cabin. It is only 16 feet wide and 18 feet long—hardly palatial. There is no piece of furniture in it worth more than 100 dollars or so. Envision *Lifestyles of the Rich and Famous*— then dash to the opposite end of the spectrum and you'll be pretty close. Yet the comments that I hear when folks see it for the first time are, "Can I just stay here forever?" or, "You know, this is all a person really needs." Could it be that the more our world becomes technologically advanced, the more peaceful "untechnologically advanced" will feel to us? Could this be part of the reason why primitive, homey, worn articles and edifices continue to increase in demand and value?

Principles of Design

There are timeless, universal visual principles that have
existed throughout the history of mankind. These
principles, if used by someone who understands them, will
make any visual item pleasing to the human eye. Most of
us do not know their names, nor even realize that we are
seeing applications of these principles, yet something in
our brains recognizes them. For thousands of years, people
have studied these principles. They were known amongst
the ancient Greeks and Romans, and in ancient Egyptian
and American cultures. They were rediscovered during the
Renaissance and the Age of Enlightenment by men like
Palladio and Thomas Jefferson. Therein we find the link to
Early American architecture. While the humble, hewn-log
home of an early Kentucky settler or the timber-framed
structures of New England may seem very far removed
from the Parthenon, these structures share many common

design features, because those who influenced the architectural styles of their eras, such as
Palladio and Jefferson, were aware of these classic principles. Though a farmer in backwoods
Maine or Pennsylvania 200 years ago may not have known the principles by name, he was
aware of the prevailing architectural styles and built his structures in accordance. Today
we recognize those principles in use amongst early American settlers, and they are just as
pleasing to the modern eye as they were 200 (or even 2,000) years ago.

Personality

One of the joys of living in a country home is the creativity involved in taking something
old and giving it new life as something else. My wife Johnna is particularly adept at finding
clever uses for an old galvanized farm-animal feeder or a beat-up, homely container, turning
it into a delightful centerpiece on the dining room table or an ingenious office organizer.

Many of the homes in this book are wonderful examples of the creative resurrection of common, simple items. In addition, much of what you'll see in these pages has been built with reused and restored materials such as logs, timbers, and miscellaneous pieces of lumber. With the recent push toward "green" construction and more conscientious stewardship of our world's natural resources, one would be hard-pressed to find a practice that consumes less than the act of reusing an existing (and often considered spent) item. The double bonus is that the object will not add to the overflowing refuse management problems of our modern existence. And old things have a patina—they tell stories.

A worn door handle or a 200-year-old hand-hewn beam has so much more personality than any new thing ever could.

Connections to the Past

We all have family ties that are deeply embedded somewhere deep inside of us. For many of us, surrounding ourselves with objects from the past helps us make intangible connections more tangible. Using items with a unique history is a way that we can connect with those who went before us—those who often sacrificed much so that we could enjoy our lives today. Using a table that belonged to a grandmother, displaying a quilt that was made during the Civil War, or, in my case, something as simple as using my grandfather's vise in my toolshed, keeps those people alive in our minds and our hearts. Perhaps that connection to our past is why, for many of us, living in Early American surroundings helps us feel . . . well, more at *home*.

I hope you enjoy this visual trek through these wonderful Early American country homes.

Generations *of* Living

RESTORED ORIGINALS

Connected to the Past

Libbey Home,
York County, Maine

ca. 1770

It is the quintessential New England experience: driving through winding backroads of beautiful deciduous forests, the smell of musty oak and hemlock, with 200-year-old stone fences and white church houses on town greens—to arrive at the home of Roger and Sylvia Libbey. Records date members of the Libbey family in the area back to the 1690s. Many generations of Libbeys were born within walking distance of here. Prior to purchasing the old family home, Roger and Sylvia had lived their entire married life in another old home—the same one where Sylvia had spent her childhood.

Roger has memories of their current residence from the time that he was a young boy, when it belonged to a cousin, Vernor. Amazingly, only two families have occupied the home throughout its existence. A family named Hardison were the original inhabitants, owning a gristmill and sawmill a few hundred yards away that date to 1774. The Libbey

A guest bedroom in the Libbey home, with furniture
original to the early 1800s.

family purchased the property in 1849, with Roger and Sylvia now being the sixth generation of Libbeys to inhabit the old, wonderful dwelling, known in New England parlance as an "extended cape."

New England wouldn't be New England without its stone fences and colonial homes.

Cousin Vernor one day related to Roger that he hated to think of what would happen to the old homestead after he was gone. Roger offered that day to purchase it and be its caretaker—then went home and told Sylvia about their new residence!

Roger and Sylvia have, in the ensuing years, completed a major renovation of the home from the ground up. Structural concerns were addressed. Fireplaces were rebuilt using original materials. Doors and windows have been restored to their earlier configurations. Post-1770 walls were removed. Exterior clapboards and interior plastering was restored. Original woodwork and flooring were mostly intact and simply needed repairs or paint. What was once a crude, dirt-floored woodshed now houses modern plumbing. A pre-1770 saltbox addition—moved from another location—was also restored.

"I often think of and feel gratitude for Vernor and his predecessors in this home—if it wasn't for them, we wouldn't have the joy that it brings to us now," said Roger. "I think of them walking across these floors, living in this space, and I feel an indescribable connection to them." It is certain that the Libbey ancestors would feel gratitude as well for Roger and Sylvia's homage to them: their current stewardship for this special home.

Three articles of cabinetry are original to the home (though they weren't here when Roger and Sylvia purchased the home). This interesting mustard-colored piece is one of them.

A view of the David T. Smith kitchen in the Libbey Home. You will see many examples of David's work throughout this book.

The hearth in the keeping room— complete with bake oven and fireplace crane. Countless hours were spent, centuries ago, cooking at this hearth.

The Libbey kitchen is one of the most famous works of David T. Smith. It was inspired by an early 1800s kitchen original to Maine, yet found in Atlanta, Georgia.

Left: This cabinet is original to the home. Six generations of the Libbey family have opened and closed these doors.

A Colonial Tavern

Bonin Home (Samuel Waters Tavern),
Sutton, Massachusetts

ca. 1775

The Samuel Waters Tavern is a remarkable little piece of history tucked into the center of New England, fronting one of the many old turnpikes common to Massachusetts. The tavern was constructed around 1775 by Mr. Samuel Waters and his wife Prudence. The property was used not only as a tavern and a private residence, but at one time in its history it was also used as a meeting house for a local group of Freemasons.

The quaint New England home has been a witness to colorful history throughout its more than 235 years of existence, including the residence of a pair of "maiden ladies" and a noted woman suffragist, Lucy Phelps. Lucy's signature can still be found on many of the walls in the upstairs ballroom of the tavern.

Bill and Cheryl Bonin grew up in neighboring areas not far from Sutton. While Cheryl was growing up, her family also resided in West Virginia for a period, in an old Victorian

The old millrace still runs through the property, leading to the site of what once was a gristmill. The original gristmill is long gone, unfortunately, but a new outbuilding, used for storage and occasional antique sales, has replaced it.

farmhouse. There she grew to appreciate the antique woodwork, unique character, and comfortable ambiance of a historic structure. As an adult, Cheryl returned to New England, married Bill, and soon became an avid collector of antiques. As time passed, her primitive antique collection grew, and their 1970s house grew more and more out of place. Cheryl longed for an old home to complete the picture, and in 2006, Bill, Cheryl, and daughter Alex were able to find the perfect structure to house the primitive antique collection—the old Samuel Waters Tavern.

The home had been favorably owned and restored by carpenter David Stevenson, who had done a fantastic job of bringing it back to its wonderful original condition. The only major part of the home that he hadn't gotten to was the kitchen. Kitchens are always somewhat tricky in an antique home—our modern cooking methods and appliances simply weren't in use 200 years ago. Fortunately, Cheryl had done much research over the years and was aware of many craftsmen around the country, particularly the Workshops of David T. Smith. As you've seen in other homes in this book, David is extremely talented at devising modern kitchens that fit perfectly into period settings. His vision, Cheryl states, was the perfect crowning element for the old tavern.

Left: The reconverted Tavern Room. This room was more than likely the original tavern, so the Bonin's have restored it to reflect that—adding in the left corner a cage bar that would have been typical in colonial times.

Right: Since most of the Bonin family meals are eaten at the table in the kitchen/keeping room, the main dining room is usually kept decorated with old tavern decor—a great way to display a wonderful collection of antiques.

The fireplace in the keeping room (part of the kitchen).

Another amazing example of David T. Smith's excellent work. Not only is the kitchen "way more functional!" (in Cheryl's words), but it also appears to have always been part of the original colonial structure.

Right: An original fireplace. Though restored, this fireplace has probably changed very little from how it appeared 200-plus years ago.

European Roots

Janke Home (Marinus Peterson Home), Sanpete County, Utah

ca. 1875

The story of Lothar (pronounced Lo-tar) and Anita Janke's home in Sanpete County, Utah is a singularly unique story involving much more than just a simple house. It is a heartwarming story of adversity and perseverance, difficulties and joys, and begs for more than just a couple of brief pages in this book. This simple, sturdy stone structure is symbolic of the quiet, graceful simplicity found among many early settlers of our nation, qualities that on occasion still can be found in our present world, amongst wonderful people such as Lothar and Anita.

Lothar and Anita were born and raised in East Germany. Their life in East Germany was not without its challenges, and the story of their departure from behind the Iron Curtain and emigration to Utah is a fascinating one. One of the Jankes' dreams in their new homeland was to have an old-time farmstead, which would also allow Anita's love for gardening to

Simple yet dignified—this old stone home will forever be stylish, and its size makes it forever quaint.

A simple, quaint corner of the dining room.

flourish. A friend, interior designer Scott Anderson, introduced them to the old stone homes of the Sanpete Valley.

Marinus Peterson, a Danish immigrant convert to the LDS faith, built this house of stone around 1875. It is an almost textbook example of a simple stone structure: basic and symmetrical, yet graceful and classic in its lines.

The Janke home has several original farm buildings on the lot: a barn, a granary, an outhouse, and a chicken coop (now converted to guest quarters for housing grandchildren). The home had a kitchen, added onto the original stone structure in about 1925, yet the entire structure needed a good restoration. The Jankes removed old wallpaper and carpeting, revealing original flooring. Old plaster and woodwork was repaired and restored. The staircase had been removed, but Anita and daughter Helena rediscovered the original location while removing modernizations, and Lothar rebuilt the staircase. The old stone house has been given new life—yet with a wonderful collection of simple antiques, this new life resembles very much its original life. The home, while Early American in style, has a definite European influence throughout. It is simple and honest, yet graceful and dignified—a wonderful reflection of Lothar and Anita.

Original and reproduction furnishings blend seamlessly throughout the home, creating a soft, wonderful atmosphere. Note the eye-pleasing paint treatment on the walls.

Above: One of the joys of having old exposed beams in a home is that one can then add authentic country touches to the decor—like these baskets. The beams then become part of the composition, and therefore part of a well-designed structure.

This old log barn was also original to the property, housing countless animals over the years. It is now the setting for annual barn dances!

Left: The staircase had been removed and covered up at one time; Lothar and Anita rebuilt it true to Early American—and European—forms.

Twist of Fate

Jense Home (Reddick Newton Allred Home), Sanpete County, Utah

ca. 1870

Once in a great while, on very rare occasions, something happens in a person's life that completely changes it. Such was the case when Sara Jense stopped to investigate an old dilapidated house one day. Sara cannot say for sure what prompted her to investigate the old structure. It was obviously in disrepair, and former owners had significantly altered the historical nature and value of the home. As she stepped onto the back porch, she noticed a small plaque mounted on the stone that read "Reddick Newton Allred House—built in 1870." Sara knew at that pivotal moment that her life was about to change, and that somehow she would own the old stone structure, for the name on the plaque was a very familiar name: Reddick Newton Allred was an ancestor of Sara's.

When Sara first purchased the old stone house, her friends questioned her level of sanity. The old home was in severe disrepair, and previous "improvements" were less than tasteful.

The kitchen was a necessary add-on for comfortable modern living, but was tastefully done to emulate and complement the original parts of the house. Reclaimed old brick was used on the floor and new cabinets were made, but in Early American style. The exposed stone wall (formerly an exterior wall) is a wonderfully welcome antique aspect of this kitchen.

She embarked on the journey of restoring the old stone home in February 1996. Every step had to be approved by the Utah State Historical Society, so the process was not simple. Yet Sara felt a responsibility for stewardship of the old structure, and was extremely painstaking about preserving the priceless historical character of the home while converting it to modern livability.

The classic Vernacular Greek Revival styling of this stone home conveys a strong sense of order and simplicity.

When the home was structurally restored, Sara set about furnishing it with mid-1800s antiques, and any reproductions that were used have been meticulously handcrafted to fit that earlier era as well. The small, quaint scale of the home created its own challenges, so much of the handcrafted furniture is custom-built at smaller-than-normal scale. Hand-spun and handwoven fabrics abound. All lighting fixtures were handmade specifically for the home. Exposed woodwork has been painted in period colors, inspired by Sara's collection of M. A. Hadley pottery from Louisville, Kentucky. Sara fortunately had been exposed to many examples of Early American architecture and interiors over the years, so her impeccable tastes have created a most wonderful dwelling.

The old Reddick Newton Allred Home now stands, humble yet stately. Its solid stone Vernacular Greek Revival–style walls echo the solid, hardy pioneers from whom Sara descended.

Right: An example of the quiet symmetry common to the Vernacular Greek Revival style. Sara had all of the light fixtures custom-made to fit this home. Her simple furnishings and wonderful collections fit the old house perfectly.

A guest room in Sara's old stone house. It would be extremely difficult to create a space that says "home" more than this example of Early American styling.

Right: A quaint and cozy sitting room. The couch was custom-made to fit the scale of this space, as were other pieces of furniture in the room.

West Virginia Mountain Cottage

Smith Cottage (Leafie's Cottage), Original Portion, Southern West Virginia

ca. mid-1800s

West Virginia is well known for its rugged mountains and spectacular scenery, as well as the hardy pioneer stock who settled its secluded valleys. Among the descendants of these hardy forebears in the mountains of West Virginia was Leafie Lilly Harvey. Leafie rode on horseback to this property the day she got married in 1923, and lived here for the rest of her life. The home's original structure predates the Civil War, but had been added onto over the years to create a wonderful, quaint, homey cottage.

When Lora Smith was a young girl, she would pass by Leafie's house each day on her way to school. Lora and Leafie were distant relatives, and Lora had a particular fondness for the quaint little cottage surrounded by the high West Virginia mountains. Lora grew up, moved to Ohio, and married David T. Smith. David and Lora eventually formed the famous Workshops of David T. Smith—a village of shops and a group of extremely talented artisans

What do you get when you combine the furnishing talents of David T. Smith, a quaint little cottage kitchen, and Lora's mouthwatering cakes and pies? Let's just say that we stayed much longer than we had intended to!

who make furniture, chairs, custom period kitchens, and handmade redware pottery. David's specialty is his wonderfully designed kitchens. Many more amazing examples of David's work are sprinkled throughout this book.

What could be more inviting than a cottage with a wraparound porch?

When David and Lora would return to her childhood home to visit family and friends, they would again pass admiringly by the old cottage where Leafie had made her home, and Lora would yearn to someday have such a cottage. In 2006, Lora was blessed with an opportunity to own Leafie's cottage. The rest, to quote Lora, "is history!—that, and a whole lot of work!"

Several years of hard work later, including gutting and restoring, and the cottage is once again a beautiful place, rich in history and warmly inviting. The home houses a wonderful collection of articles from the skilled hands at the Workshops of David T. Smith, as well as one of David's trademark kitchens. The beadboard walls have been painted a soft, warm yellow (matched to the original paint color) throughout the house. Antiques and reproductions sit side by side, and the feeling of home permeates throughout. Lora's excellent interior design abilities are showcased in every nook and cranny of the cottage, and time spent there is simply a treat that words can barely describe.

Right: The early fireplace (made from quarried stone from the area) in this sitting room was an unexpected surprise—found in the restoration process.

Above: The earliest part of the house dates from prior to the Civil War. The two original rooms shared a central chimney. Note the small, sunny porch area converted into a light-filled office.

The living room at Leafie's Cottage—a welcoming invitation to enjoy the warm comforts of country living.

Left: The soft yellow beadboard walls and ceilings impart a warm glow to every room, as in this dining room.

Wasatch Stone

ca. 1862

Cody Wright was born about 100 years late. "I admit it," he says, "I should have been born in the 1800s—but my wife wouldn't have been too wild about that idea—so I had to live now." Cody and his wife Kari live in a remarkable old rock home at the foot of the Wasatch Mountains in Box Elder County in northern Utah. Cody is a stonemason and restorer of old homes, so it is only fitting that they live in one.

The original stone home had been owned by a Mr. Omer Call. Omer and his twin brother, Homer, were business partners in northern Utah in the second half of the nineteenth century. Together they owned and operated the county's first flour mill. In 1856, Omer helped to build freighting stations between Utah and Missouri. Omer and Homer also subcontracted many miles of road on the Union Pacific line in Wyoming and Utah. (The famous joining spot of the transcontinental railroad in 1869 lies in Box Elder County not far from here.)

This old kitchen cookstove was purchased as a pile of rusted parts. Cody restored it and had the nickel plating redone. It burns nearly nonstop during the winter months, and is often the only heat source needed. The adobe wall behind it absorbs the heat and radiates it back throughout the night.

The Call home, at times, served as a halfway house for travelers. A story is told that Mrs. Call graciously served a chicken dinner to federal marshals downstairs while several shady characters were escaping through the upstairs windows.

When Cody and Kari first purchased the home in April 2004, it was in dire need of a thorough restoration. Though the stone walls were structurally sound, just about all else was in need of repair and replacement. They gutted the structure down to stone walls and a dirt floor, and began to rebuild. "My dad [Danny Wright] was there right beside me every day!" said Cody. New floors were put in, new wiring and plumbing installed, and plastered walls were restored. The process all sounds simple when condensed down to a few sentences, but the transformation took a year from starting until moving in, "—and I'm still at it!" Cody adds.

There is a definite sense of accomplishment when one takes the labors of those from the past and brings new life and love to them. One develops an intangible link to those people—much more than just admiration and appreciation. Lives become inseparably connected—even though those lives may be a century apart.

A remarkable blend of simple, early lines with just a touch of flamboyant gingerbread makes this home extremely quaint. The alpenglow of northern Utah's Wasatch Mountains adds a dramatic backdrop to the scene.

Right: The charming, beckoning kitchen—always a space where family loves to gather.

Bathrooms are often a challenge in old homes, yet can also be one of the most intriguing spaces. This spacious bath is the work of Kari Wright—charming and very inviting. Owners of Cody and Kari's previous home had buried this tub into the ground and used it as a flower planter. The Wrights dug it up and saved it from that horrible embarrassment—restoring it to its former proud self.

Right: The master bedroom with an eclectic collection of antiques. One of the benefits of antique homes is that owners can pick and choose the type of antiques they like best. Some choose to adhere to a certain period, while others simply use what appeals to them, regardless of period. There is no right or wrong to Early American style.

Adding *to* History

RESTORED ORIGINALS WITH MODERN ADDITIONS

Pioneer Tenacity

ca. 1865

Central Utah, and specifically Sanpete County, is a unique location in the western United States. Much of the West was settled in the Victorian period, so there are few places where one can see simple homes common to Georgian, Federal, or Greek Revival styles. Yet sleepy little Sanpete County houses a remarkable number of homes built in the simple Early American style. One of the most notable is a wonderful stone home owned by Bruce and Bonnie Barker—notable because it is an excellent example of Vernacular Greek Revival style, because it has been carefully, meticulously, and lovingly restored, and because the original owner was a prominent figure in early Utah and Mormon history.

Orson Hyde, born in 1805 in Oxford, Connecticut, was an early leader in what many refer to as the Mormon church (actually named the Church of Jesus Christ of Latter-day Saints, or LDS Church). LDS Church members in the early nineteenth century were the recipients

This antique sofa was built by Anders Swenson around 1870.
Swenson was a Scandinavian Mormon immigrant, a cabinetmaker
by trade whose work is now highly collectible.

This simple but stately limestone home once belonged to early Mormon pioneer leader Orson Hyde. This house is an excellent example of classic architectural principles in use among Early American pioneer settlers.

of severe persecution in upstate New York, Ohio, Missouri, and Illinois. Thus the Mormon people sought refuge in the Rocky Mountains. Orson Hyde eventually settled in the Sanpete Valley of central Utah, building this oolitic limestone home—a standing testament to pioneer tenacity and frontier dangers. Gun ports in the cellar of the old stone granary, now used by the Barkers as a guesthouse, are lingering evidence of Utah's Black Hawk War of the late 1860s.

In May 2002 the Barkers visited the Sanpete area and happened upon an ad indicating that the "Orson Hyde Homestead" was for sale. Soon they became the 14th owners of the property. The home had been somewhat structurally maintained throughout most of its history, but was badly in need of major repairs and a restoration by someone with an appreciative eye for Early American simplicity. The Barkers were the perfect stewards for the historic property. Previous remodels by owners who had little zeal for history were undone and more appropriate decisions were made. A beautiful country kitchen was added on in the place of older, irreparable additions, and Bruce and Bonnie have furnished it with early Mormon antiques and collections. The result of the exceptional efforts of the Barkers is a wonderful, warm, and homey example of period architecture, with the sturdy, stately stone walls standing as a testament to pioneer lives.

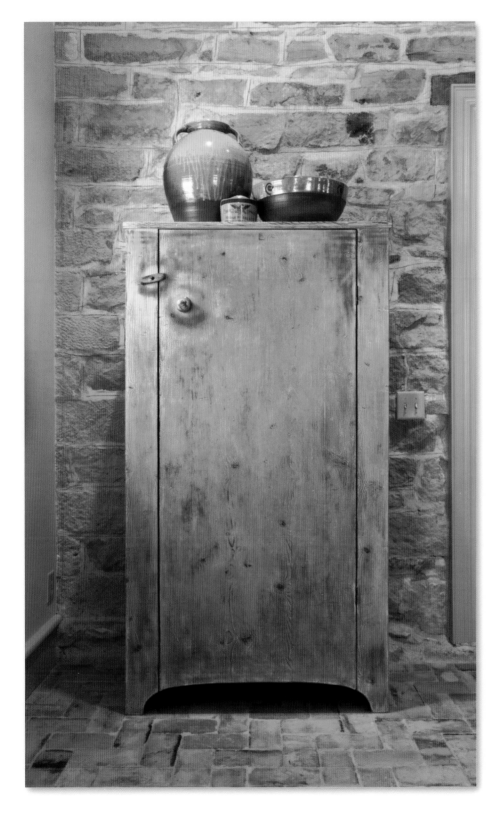

The back lean-to reveals the
added charm of the stone wall
on what was previously the back
of the house. The reproduction
cabinet was made by local
craftsman Dale Peel.

Previous remodels had created less-than-ideal bathroom spaces. The Barkers created this warm and cozy bathroom space, modern in function but appearing as from the past.

Right: A modest but inviting country dining room, ready for entertaining visitors. Note the excellent examples of grain painting on the door, and the patina of hand-restored floors.

A Connecticut Yankee

ca. 1784–1810

There is something extremely special about an original old New England home that words simply can't describe. Such is the case with Larry and Sandy Neary's home in Litchfield County, Connecticut. Some records show the house being built in 1794, while the family bible of the original owners mentions a date of 1810. At one time in its history the home was in such bad shape that it was actually condemned. Yet previous owners had cared for the property and had begun the painstaking process of restoring it to its former quaint stateliness.

Sandy relates that they loved the home the first moment they peered into the wavy glass windows on a February evening in 1978, knowing at the time that it was vacant—but for sale. They could make out a little fireplace in the kitchen, and the home called to them. The structure was still in very rugged shape, and the roofline sported waves like the Atlantic

One of the portions of the home that has been so tastefully added on is
the master bedroom. The wonderful painted mantle is old material—
reused in a creative way. Also creative is the slightly whimsical floor
paint—based on Early American decorative styling.

Quintessential New England—complete with stone wall and autumn leaves.

Ocean in a storm, but the Nearys could see the jewel that most people couldn't.

Both Larry and Sandy had grown up with an appreciation for old homes, and were ready to tackle the remaining restoration needed. Knowing that the home would be too small in which to raise their children—now grown Kate and Tucker—they have, over time, meticulously added two extensions to the home, being careful to maintain the historic look and feel. Materials came from all over New England—including original mantles, old brick, and antique flooring and beams—scrounged up by the Nearys on their forays through the countryside.

Larry and Sandy have filled their home with wonderful antiques—some are family heirlooms, others have been purchased over the years. For example, Sandy has a photo of a beloved great aunt seated in a small wooden Victorian child's chair—the photo is displayed near the actual chair in the Neary Home. It is obvious that the Neary Home has been a labor of much love over the years. Sandy talks of her home that "wraps its arms around you" with a twinkle in her eyes, and Larry commented that, "The whole experience has been like finding your old pair of slippers you'd forgotten you had."

This parlor is cozy but a bit more formal—great for small groups, or often used as an additional room when moving about during an evening of entertaining. It also makes a perfect, quiet retreat.

Above: The dining room in Larry and Sandy Neary's colonial home, complete with one of several original, restored fireplaces.

Although the Nearys have added on to the original structure over the years, they have wonderfully maintained the original colonial look of the home. One cannot easily tell, inside or out, whether one is looking at original home or artful augmentations.

Right: Though part of an addition, this gathering room still retains the ambiance of the original home with its uneven plank floors, and salvaged mantle, bricks, and hewn beams.

Old Kentucky Home

Sayre Home,
Midway, Kentucky

ca. 1880

I am incredibly fond of Kentucky. I love the rolling terrain, the dark-stained board fences and stone walls, the indescribable horse farms, the amazing natural beauty, and the frontier history. Midway, Kentucky is surrounded by just what I've described. A main street lined with charming shops and restaurants greets the visitor to Midway. It is no wonder that Tom and Mary Sayre have settled in this wonderful little area of Thoroughbred racehorse heaven—Kentucky's Bluegrass Region. Tom was born in Kentucky "and will die in Kentucky!" says Mary, with a tone of obvious resoluteness. Mary was lured to Kentucky in her youth when her uncle promised that he'd buy her a horse.

The quaint little cottage home of Tom and Mary was originally built in 1880 on a farm located outside of town, but was moved into town in 1908. Tom and Mary were immediately enchanted by the cottage, with the front porch columns and nineteenth-century clapboard

An exceptional kitchen from David T. Smith—this one is slightly different from others that you've seen in this book. The Sayre kitchen has a distinct cottage feel to it, inspired by the original.

The Sayre front porch welcomes visitors in the charming little town of Midway, Kentucky.

exterior. Original heart pine flooring, three fireplaces, and wonderful old woodwork had them even more captivated. On one side of the home, the town of Midway can be viewed through the windows. The other side of the home looks out over the rolling countryside and pastoral fields—complete with grazing cattle—in this exceptional little corner of Kentucky.

The story is told that a heinous crime had been committed at the Parrish Farm where the house originally stood. It would have been another crime for Tom and Mary to have not purchased the little cottage. In 2002 they bought it and began an extensive renovation project, as well as adding on to the structure. The Sayres wanted to make sure that any addition would fit with the style of the home, so were extremely careful to add on in a matching historic style. A family room, porch, and master bedroom suite were added to the rear portion of the home. A marvelous David T. Smith kitchen now replaces the expanded original, the design of which Mary and David collaborated on.

Mary owns a wonderful little antiques shop, May and Company, within walking distance of their home (Mary's maiden name is May—hence the name). She and Tom have a wonderful collection of antiques—Tom is especially fond of antique windmill weights, waterfowl decoys, and horseracing and baseball memorabilia.

A child's bed tucked lovingly into a dormer
space under the eaves—complete with
trundle bed. This charming room is a
favorite of visiting children.

The French doors in the family room addition open onto the beautiful bluegrass countryside and breathtaking Kentucky sunsets.

Left: The vaulted ceiling in the study was a happy accident: when a reroofing job damaged the existing ceiling, Tom and Mary decided to make it a vaulted ceiling instead. The room displays some of Tom and Mary's large collection of antiques, including carved wooden decoys and old baskets.

Western Reserve Farmhouse

ca. 1880

Every once in a great while something bad turns to something good. Such was the case in 1978, when northeastern Ohio experienced the Blizzard of '78. Snow piled high and caused extensive damage to the area. This eventually became a good thing for Paul and Toni Willmott, for Toni's brother told them of an old farmhouse near his home that was damaged by the storm—and therefore available for sale. Paul and Toni had been considering moving to the countryside, where their three young boys (eventually four) might be able to roam the fields and woods with relative freedom. The old farmhouse sat on a 40-acre lot in part of Ohio known as the Connecticut Western Reserve.

The home had been built around 1880. Paul and Toni were the fifth owners since that time, the structure having undergone several changes in its history. Unfortunately, quite a few of the original parts of the structure had been removed over time in an effort to modernize

This breakfast nook off the kitchen is permeated with Early American styling: old hand-hewn beams, wide plank flooring, period colors, and reproduction lighting and furnishings. One of the incredibly wonderful parts about living in today's world is that we can have breakfast nooks—definitely modern areas—that appear to be 200 years old.

it. Fortunately, inside the old barn on the property Paul and Toni discovered many of the missing pieces of the house. Doors that had been replaced over time were stored there, as were trim, moldings, and shutters.

Paul has been a home builder since he and Toni were first married, and although he still does new construction on a regular basis, his forte is actually the restoration of or additions

to antique structures. Paul has an extremely good eye for bringing unique old buildings (and additions to them) back to their former glory. For these projects, Paul often acquires original building materials from Denny Walker, who is mentioned several times elsewhere in this book.

One of the most notable points about this home is that though the exterior is extremely charming,

While most of the homes in this book lean toward simpler styles, this home is so amazingly quaint that I could not resist including it. Classic design is always a treat for the eye—whether simple, or charmingly ornate like this example.

Paul and Toni prefer a more primitive interior space. So with amazing ingenuity, they've made it appear that the house was added on to over time (as is often typical of old homes), with later nineteenth-century portions being added onto a more primitive early nineteenth-century dwelling, when the reality is exactly the opposite.

The restoration of the Willmott house took place gradually over several years. Yet with time, Paul and Toni have brought the home back to its original graces—and have made significant historical improvements especially suited to modern living along the way.

Paul and Toni's kitchen is extremely inviting
and cozy—yet spacious at the same time. One of
the best things about taking pictures of old house
interiors, for a photographer and author, is that
owners prepare for your arrival with pies and
other goodies used as props.

One travels from a late-1800s scene into this early-1800s setting as one progresses through the home. This somewhat primitive scene would never have been constructed in 1880, yet blends seamlessly with the existing structure—a testament to Paul and Toni's exceptional abilities and tastes.

Right: Upon entering the home, one is greeted by this more formal parlor or living room. This room feels as if it belongs to the exterior of the building, but is also slightly simplified—to gradually transition one toward the rear portions of the home.

Kentucky Horse Heaven

Walden Home (Paul's Mill), Woodford County, Kentucky

ca. 1790–1813

Kentucky is perhaps most famous for its Bluegrass Region and world-renowned horseracing industry. The equestrian facilities in this part of the nation are some of the most beautiful in the world. Yet, as we drove down the lane of the Woodford County farm known as Paul's Mill, we commented to each other about the singular beauty of this particular farm. I suppose there might be farms that are more affluent or lavish, but the setting at Paul's Mill has to be one of the most spectacular in the state of Kentucky.

There are several records of a "John Paul" in early Kentucky, and it is not known if they record one person or several, but it is certain that by 1813 John Paul owned and operated a gristmill on Clear Creek, near the community of Troy (now in Woodford County). The stone mill house was either existing or built at this time. The John Paul family also built several other structures on the property, including two barns, a log corncrib, a distillery, and

The Shaker-style cabinetry in the second-floor office area of the old mill house. Occasionally, one has to pull oneself away from the incredible Kentucky scenic view through the windows to watch a horse race on the big-screen TV, located behind the upper cabinet doors. Chances are you'll see a Paul's Mill resident win, place, or show. Summer Bird, winner of the final jewel of the triple crown in 2009—the Belmont Stakes—stands at stud here.

brick slave quarters. Other local families developed a sawmill, a blacksmith shop, and an inn to accommodate visitors bringing wood, grain, and corn to the mills, creating a small but thriving community during the nineteenth century.

Several owners have added improvements to and renovated the property over the years, but the restoration of the property to its historic character has mostly occurred since 2008, when Ben and Elaine Walden purchased the property as the location for their outstanding Thoroughbred racehorse farm. Ben and Elaine have undertaken to restore Paul's Mill to its historic graces, starting with the restoration of its name. The old stone mill house has been restored and is one of the few Woodford County buildings on the National Register of Historic Places. It is again the center of a bustling business, with the farm offices located inside. Old wooden gristmill gears sit side by side with state-of-the-art computer technology, yet the two blend together beautifully.

The restored stone gristmill house, now the offices for the Paul's Mill racehorse operation. One slight improvement has been made to the historic quality of the structure: a bank of windows on each gable end allows a view of the incredible Kentucky countryside and wooded creek bottoms.

Many of the buildings on the property have also undergone restoration under Ben's direction, and the Waldens talk of further restoration plans. "Paul's Mill has been kept so beautifully by its past owners," Ben says. "We want to continue in that tradition. It is a very special place."

Inside the stone mill house, among the original hewn beams and plank floors, David T. Smith does it again with this wonderful kitchen—always so tasteful, always just right.

Another view of David T. Smith's magic. The sink is constructed of soapstone in a style authentic to the 1800–1810 era, while providing completely modern functionality. The black cabinet at right is the refrigerator.

Left: The Walden Home is rich with history. Built about 1813 by John Paul, it now is a comfortable dwelling place for Ben, Elaine, and daughter Hope.

Creating Timelessness

NEW HOMES WITH ORIGINAL MATERIALS

Blue Ridge Vision

Bradley Home (Moriah),
Earlysville, Virginia

ca. 2008

Noah H. Bradley III began his carpentry career at the ripe old age of 15, under the tutelage of his father, working with salvaged materials years before the trend became popular. Over the years he had the opportunity to work for several master craftsmen, learning all the ins and outs of modern as well as early construction. Along the way, Noah developed a vision of building that incorporates the best of both worlds—timeless designs and antique materials combined with modern comfort and efficiency. In 1988, Noah and Lynne formed the company Blue Mountain Builders with this vision in mind. They specialize in creating timeless homes and cabins using antique hand-hewn beams and logs, homes that emanate the warm, cozy feeling of old dwellings yet perform as well as new construction.

Back in the mid-1970s, a wealthy woman near Charlottesville, Virginia with impeccable tastes and a love of old materials amassed a crew of excellent craftsmen and acquired several

A quaint corner in the kitchen, complete with a working flour mill.

period buildings in the area from which a new home would be built. Her choices in materials old and new were second to none. The crew built a home that became an early example of a movement Noah would later refine with his vision of combining the best of old and new.

A view of the postcard-perfect Blue Ridge Mountains of Albemarle County that envelope Moriah.

Several years ago, new owners came along who had little appreciation for the historical materials combined in this home. Noah knew of their value, and was given the opportunity to purchase the structure, but not the property. He purchased the building and dismantled it, not really knowing where it would eventually end up. In time, Noah and Lynne found an absolutely beautiful piece of property in Albemarle County, and decided to use those treasured materials to construct their own home. The property sits on a knoll, surrounded by gently rolling, postcard-perfect countryside and bordered on two sides by a clear Blue Ridge Mountain stream. They knew this would be the perfect spot for these unique materials and this wonderful home. Now, hewn timbers and log walls with a warm patina greet the visitor to a wonderful, cozy ambiance not usually found in a home of this generous size. Modern amenities blend effortlessly with the aged materials. The home is bright and airy, yet encircles one like a soft blanket. Lynne and Noah have christened their home with the name "Moriah."

Part of the home consists of an old hewn-log cabin—made into a stunning dining room by Noah and his artisans.

The breakfast nook in the kitchen looks
out over the surrounding countryside
and down to the clear mountain stream
that flows through the property.

Right: Above the dining room in the
old cabin part of the home, a cozy
guest bedroom awaits visitors.

Ridges of
Madison County

ca. 1995/2002

About two hours southwest from Washington, D.C., lies a sleepy little county where rolling hills and wonderful old farms dot the landscape. Virginia is a beautiful state, with many splendid areas, but Madison County is an especially alluring place. Although Bill and Marise Craig both grew up and had spent much of their married life in northern Virginia, they had long been enamored of the idyllic farms and lovely rural landscape of the area. In 1990, they purchased their own little corner of Madison County, with the idea of building a small vacation home where family could get together.

The Craigs met local builder Noah Bradley of Blue Mountain Builders, who specializes in the restoration and reproduction of classic early Virginia homes and cabins. As the Craigs visited with Noah, they became convinced that a historic structure would be ideal for the setting. Noah found a quaint little building—half of an old log barn—and Blue Mountain Builders

The connector between the original log cabin and the newer main house is the perfect location for this spacious dining room. A bay window not only allows a view of the splendid countryside, but is also the ideal place for a collection of antique salt-glazed stoneware jugs.

Main house and cabin are artfully bridged with a stone connection. As was done in the past, the home has been added onto as the need arose over time.

constructed the perfect getaway cabin. So perfect, in fact, that Bill and Marise knew exactly when the time came a few years ago where they wanted to spend their retirement years. Thus, in 2000 the Craigs contacted Noah Bradley again. The little cabin could simply not be added onto by just anyone! An addition—the main house—was begun the following summer and completed nearly a year later.

The synthesis of the Craig family with Noah Bradley and his crew has yielded a wonderful treasure in the Blue Ridge Mountains of Virginia. One visitor remarked after an informal tour, "Don't these rooms just wrap their arms around you?" It is obvious that Bill and Marise love their home and love living in Madison County. "We've never been emotionally attached to a structure before—until we lived here."

Family treasures abound in the Craig Home. Photos from bygone ancestors dot many of the walls. Heirlooms and remarkable antiques are in abundance. Marise can tell story after story of the genealogical history of each cherished item. Long-gone loved ones feel comfortably close at hand. Future generations connect to reality here. The Craig Home is warm and enchanting, another marvelous example of the feeling of "home" in an Early American dwelling.

The living room, showing the wonderful old hewn
beams of an earlier dwelling. These beams would
be covered up in the original structure, yet Noah
Bradley envelops them with modern walls to
showcase their unique, rugged beauty. The green
on the walls is inspired by a green jasperware
Wedgwood pendant given to Marise by Bill upon
the occasion of their high school graduation.

The sitting room in the original cabin.
The Craigs have collected antiques since
they were first married—everywhere
there are treats for the eyes.

*Right: A corner of Bill's office
under the eaves—one would
be hard-pressed to find a cozier
working space.*

Family Traits

ca. 2005

Early American antique homes, perfect candidates for restoration, do not always sit where they need to be. Ryan and Ali Grubbs knew that they wanted a restored hewn-log home, yet they owned property next door to Ryan's parents, and desired to have their children grow up near extended family. Although there are wonderful historic homes in central Kentucky, there was not one in the exact location they desired to live. Thus, rather than going to the house, they brought the house to their site.

When Ryan was a young boy, his father built a home for their family from reclaimed antique hewn logs. He grew up with the idea that someday he would restore an antique log structure for his own family. Ali had grown up in a home where her family had a deep appreciation for antiques. She loved visiting Ryan's family in their cozy, comfortable old log home, and was easily convinced when Ryan proposed the idea of building something similar.

What better place to "sit back and relax a spell"?

97

With time and patience, the Grubbs found two log cabins nearby and another in Tennessee for use in building their dream home. They dismantled the structures and began the process of putting them back together, aided by local carpenter Bill Ward. Ryan's father and other extended family joined in, too. Along with the logs, they salvaged other materials, such as the mantles in the dining area and master bedroom, and the stones for the fireplaces.

Ali's aunt introduced them to kitchen designer David T. Smith, who could create the perfect complement to the old logs—maintaining the historic ambiance while being completely efficient and useful for modern cooking needs. You've seen David's work elsewhere and often in this book; his work is unequalled in replicating the old finishes and patina of Early American furnishings.

Middle Kentucky and Tennessee are well known for the unique style of hewn-log construction known as a "dog trot."

The overall effect is that one has stepped back in time into a perfectly restored antique hewn-log home—one in which the original builders were amazingly adept at foreseeing what future homeowners would need. It is warm and comfortable, spacious yet cozy, lovingly old but usefully new—the perfect setting to raise a young family, next door to grandparents, nestled amongst woods and fields, and literally surrounded by rich Kentucky history, even down to the very walls of the dwelling.

Above: The simple, extremely cozy master bedroom.

Left: This dining room is an amazing example of the charm, livability, and rustic beauty of Early American style.

This sitting area in the master bedroom is made all the more wonderful with an antique mantle and hearthstones salvaged from the original cabins.

Left: The magic of David T. Smith is evident in this wonderful kitchen— the perfect complement to a historic hewn-log country home.

Italianate Virginia

O'Connor Home (Western
View), Madison County, Virginia

ca. 1998

When one has a love for old homes, it is hard to imagine settling for a new, modern home. Modern homes are convenient and all, but they never seem to be able to match the warmth and ambiance of an old home. An old home feels comfortable like an old pair of slippers—soft and familiar like a favorite sweatshirt. So what does one do when an old home doesn't stand where one needs it to stand? Where an old home doesn't exist? One has to get creative, like Michael and Kathie O'Connor had to. In addition, they had to find a builder who could understand what they wanted, someone who was like-minded—someone who understood about old homes. That builder was Noah Bradley and his crew at Blue Mountain Builders. With the input of architect friend Amy Sanderson, the three parties put their heads together and came up with a truly outstanding home, nestled in the Blue Ridge Mountains of Virginia. What they created is new in function, but old in comfort—like an old friend.

Yogi always stands ready to greet visitors (or in this case, lies ready). The doorway, reclaimed from a Civil War–era hospital, was frequented by the footsteps of Walt Whitman.

Early American meets Old World in this beautiful and practical raised-hearth fireplace—inspired by kitchens of the Italian countryside.

The O'Connors lived in Rome for several years, and vacationed in Tuscany, so although the home is primarily Early American in style, it also has obvious Italian influences. Perhaps the most unusual characteristic is the wonderful raised cooking hearth inspired by homes in the Italian countryside. The fireplace is centered in the room, with the generous hearth extending along the length of the wall. This Old World treatment creates such a warm ambiance for the entire kitchen that when the O'Connors entertain, guests often spend their time sitting on the ends of the brick hearth near the crackling fire.

Two primary buildings were used to build the structure, one from nearby Culpeper, Virginia, and the other originating in Franklin, Virginia. Additional materials were gathered from several other old buildings, as well. The O'Connors joke that the house came with many ghosts, but they all seem to get along. Noah insists that his ability to be creative stems from tasteful owners who are willing to look outside of the box. "And the O'Connors," he says, "have exceptional taste!" As an example of Early American style, this home stands unique because of its Old World influences, yet it nestles comfortably in its beautiful Blue Ridge Mountain setting.

The wainscoting that you see is all original to the old homes it was salvaged from—testimony to the labor of Noah and his crew to make it fit—but that work was well worth it for the beauty that it adds to the house. Paint colors are a nice blend of Tuscany and antebellum Virginia. Note the interesting carved timber upright—salvaged from an old barn.

Left: This unique area of the house—a stair landing—came about when Noah Bradley had to join the two main antique structures and incorporate an old heart pine staircase. The result is a beautiful example of architecture—sculptural in quality.

The original artistic doors and trim work in the master bedroom were the contribution of yet another old home located near Buckingham, Virginia.

Idaho Transplant

Stukel Home,
Teton Valley, Idaho

ca. 2002

Throughout this book, you've seen several Early American antique homes that have been wonderfully restored or re-created. Most of these homes sit on or near their original locations. On occasion, however, the tastes of an owner are completely different than what he or she finds in a certain locality. In today's world, we enjoy the advantageous ability to transport materials—even entire structures—across the country. Such is the case with the Stukel home in Idaho, which my wife Johnna and I built. This hewn-log home was transported nearly 2,000 miles to its present location, a feat that would have amazed early settlers.

Johnna and I lived in Connecticut for several years. As we traveled the East Coast, enjoying the historic sites and architecture, we fell in love with the hewn-log buildings near Lancaster County, Pennsylvania. Returning to the West to be closer to family, we found a wonderful

One of the pleasant aspects of building a new structure using old
materials—a vaulted ceiling to create a slightly grander master bedroom.
This would not have been done in olden times, of course, but since we now
have the option, why not pick and choose from the best of old and new?

A sturdy, hewn-log structure, warm and inviting after a day of winter play.

wooded property—a piece of land that begged for an old, restored structure. Good fortune led us to Denny Walker of Tallmadge, Ohio, who dealt in salvaged, early historic materials. We purchased an old log structure from southeastern Ohio, and over the next year or so, Johnna and I slowly put the home together, with much help from my dad and Denny, who has become like family to us.

We loved this home so much, and thought it would be the last one that we would ever build. But I've learned in life that one can't predict the future—at least I can't. Johnna was working at the time, but we wished she could be a stay-at-home mom. One day we realized that selling the home might enable us to accomplish that. Sometimes planets just seem to align, for at the same time John and Geri Stukel happened to be looking for something old and unique in the area. Both had grown up with a love and appreciation for antiques, and had restored an old home themselves. They purchased the log home, and Johnna and I started over on a piece of adjacent land. We couldn't have picked better neighbors than John and Geri. They have since added several improvements, always being extremely meticulous about keeping the old atmosphere and creating a warm, cozy dwelling place.

Above: John and Geri have amassed numerous antiques and reproduction pieces to accent the home beautifully, like this hickory bench by the front door—a perfect place to sit down and remove one's boots!

Left: This family room was based on several original cabin homes in the eastern United States.

The timber-frame and old plank floors in this portion of the house came from an old barn in Pennsylvania. The Stukels added the incredible wood-fired pizza oven at the far end of the room. John also built the kitchen island with soapstone top.

Right: The upstairs central hallway. The beams on the ceiling are not structural, but simply added for effect. Everything not seen inside the walls, floors, and ceiling is made of new materials, and of course built to code. One can add much flavor to new construction by adding the occasional beam or other historic treatment, thereby making a home with the personality that most new homes lack.

Something Old, Something New

ORIGINAL MATERIALS AS ACCENTS

Best of Both Worlds

Miller Home,
Stark County, Ohio

ca. 1990

The story of the home of Howard and Marsha Miller is a very engaging tale, with several unusual twists and turns along the way. It is the story of a family whose tastes and preferences slowly evolved into an amazing end product. While some Early American homes, admittedly, wouldn't necessarily appeal to the masses, the Miller Home stands out as a dwelling where even those without a taste for the old would come away extremely impressed. It truly is a beautiful home. Although Howard and Marsha had an interest in antiques in earlier years, their understanding and affection for old things took time to mature. In their case, the catalyst for their refined tastes were visits to the home of Nancy Kalin, a neighbor, friend, interior designer, and restoration consultant who was a pioneer in the Early American design field.

As their tastes evolved, the desire to build a home in Early American style increased. They

Original materials abound throughout the Miller Home, like the hewn beams and period wainscoting in this room. Shutters were created to look as though they originated with the wainscoting.

considered restoring an original building from New England, but found none that met their floor-plan needs. Soon it became apparent that they might be better off to build new, but to use old materials as finish materials to gain the look they wanted. In 1988 they began

The Miller Home sits on a gentle knoll surrounded by rural Ohio countryside and the extended Miller family. The home was closely based on original New England examples.

building this "new but old" structure that would become their family home. It is situated on a beautiful knoll, part of an old farm that belonged to Howard's family.

Under the old materials lies new, modern construction, with state-of-the-art utility systems. It is in the finishing treatments that the Millers swayed drastically from modern norms. At first, reclaimed materials were planned only for the first floor—but as the home progressed, Howard and Marsha found that they loved the ambiance and personality the old materials imbued, so reclaimed materials are found throughout the entire home. Howard especially loves old stone sinks, troughs, and the like. A stone springhouse, moved from a location an hour south, serves as a garden outbuilding.

Old houses and materials are witnesses to family histories, past and present. Although they may not talk, they still tell a story. There is a sense of comfort and belonging that one feels, surrounded by the sheltering past. It's difficult to say which entity is more fortunate—the materials lovingly saved by appreciative stewards, or the family who gets to enjoy the spirit of the old materials.

Above: The original painted paneling in this room was found in two separate locations over an hour apart. Amazingly, it matched in both style and color when brought to the site!

Left: Hand-painted walls with local scenery were common in many upscale homes of New England—replicated in this remarkable dining room.

The dining room hearth, complete with antique
fireplace crane. Every detail has been so meticulously
thought out by Howard and Marsha that it is hard
to believe that one is not standing in an original
New England structure.

Above: The elegant but rustic master bedroom. Early American homes allow one to dial in on the perfect combination of warmth, homeyness, and taste.

Left: I suppose one could refer to this as a "country kitchen"—but that description would fall very short of communicating the warmth and charm of this space.

Midwestern New England

Clinch Home,
Dunlap, Illinois

ca. 1977

It is always a treat to hear lovers of Early American style talk about their homes. To many people a house is just a house, but those who have gone to all the hard work to restore or re-create historic dwellings are passionate about history and passionate about the homeyness of their dwellings. Such is the case with Rich and Jean Clinch. Their wonderful home north of Peoria, Illinois has truly been a labor of love for over 35 years. This love began long before they ever conceived of the house.

As a young couple, their first tastes in furnishings were a few antiques and Ethan Allen–type reproductions. Time spent with a college friend and her old restored farmhouse began to cement in Jean's mind that someday she would like to upgrade to more antiques or even nicer reproductions. One day she asked Rich, "What if I slowly sell what we now have, and use the funds to trade up?" Rich thought that was a great idea, and so began the process of filling their home with wonderful old antiques.

*A simple yet stately front entrance, so common in
New England, is a welcome surprise in Illinois.*

Over time they built up quite a collection, yet it seemed out of place in their Peoria ranch house. Jean had many fond recollections of her uncle and aunt's restored Cape Cod home, and of how cozy and comfortable it always felt. It became apparent that someday Rich and Jean would have a home that would match their growing antique collections. After several research trips to New England, they were ready to build.

Another masterpiece from the hand of David T. Smith. A trademark of David's kitchens is the variation of colors and a slightly different style in each cabinet—creating the look of a kitchen that has been pieced together over time.

Working with a contractor who was willing to follow their wishes closely, they began construction in the summer of 1977, and moved into the house the following winter. Over the years they have slowly and occasionally made changes, improving here and adjusting there. Because Rich and Jean are teachers, they were able to work full-time on the home in the summer months. In 1994 a significant addition was made in the form of a family room, and a David T. Smith kitchen, which the Clinches had long dreamed of, was recently added. Their home, although complete with modern conveniences, is steeped in historic New England style—the perfect place to house their wonderful antiques collections. It is hard to put into words the joy that comes from surrounding oneself with Early Americana, and the comfortable, cozy feeling that permeates the Clinch Home.

This cupboard was purchased in New Hampshire, but came from northern Maine. Note the unusual wooden hinges—indicative of early times, when iron hinges were not easily acquired, either because there was no local blacksmith or the iron hinges were simply too expensive for a frontier family.

Left: The Clinch Home is filled with example after example of wonderful old primitive cupboards such as this dry sink at left and the barn-red hutch behind it.

The fireplace in this dining area is inspired by several different hearths from original Early American homes in New England.

Greenfield Village Genesis

Edwards Home,
Southeastern Michigan

ca. 1991

The historic Henry Ford Museum and Greenfield Village in Dearborn, Michigan are a mecca for those who love history, for history comes to life so much more at a reconstructed historical site than it ever can by reading a textbook. Old Sturbridge Village, Williamsburg, Winterthur, and many other sites have stirred countless imaginations, and are a constant source of ideas for those who enjoy Early American homes.

Dan and Janet Edwards grew up in Dearborn, not far from Greenfield Village. Though not acquainted with one another at the time, each remembers forays to the Village as young schoolchildren. As they began to date one another in high school, they found their mutual love of history, and a particular admiration for the Daggett Farmhouse at the Village, to be a significant part of the common ground that eventually led to their marriage. Thus it is no surprise that years later, after many research trips to New England, they built a wonderful reproduction New England saltbox.

Bird bottles, called "Martin pots" in colonial times, were often used in colonial gardens to help with insect control. One hangs on the door of the garage—contributing to this classic colonial still-life scene.

Finding a young builder willing to follow their every admonition, Dan was on-site every day to make sure that the construction would stay true to form—true to a New England saltbox. "Contractors don't necessarily want an owner on-site," Dan said, "but this was too important to let work progress without an eye for how things should be." Dan and Janet's research and attention to detail paid off immensely. Through the years, the Edwards have finished and refinished much of the home as their tastes and knowledge became more refined.

Collections of artisans' works surround one in the Edwards Home. Many of the craftspeople have become friends of Dan and Janet's over the years.

Not only has the home evolved to become an extraordinary example of early New England architecture, it also has been transformed into a repository of the works of many of the nation's most prominent artists and artisans—with paintings of Will Moses, Janet Connor's hooked rugs, Greg Shooner's redware, a David T. Smith kitchen, and many others. Every item has a special story, and Dan and Janet have gotten to know almost every artist and artisan along the way.

The ability to pick and choose from the best of New England style has been an extraordinary asset, for it would be difficult, even in New England, to find this look all in one place. The Edwards Home is quintessential New England in a lovely corner of Michigan.

More from the Workshops of David T. Smith—another incredibly crafted period kitchen. Sink, counters, and range backsplash are made of soapstone.

This spacious master bedroom has all the
comfort and space of modern times—
and the warmth and ambiance of the
eighteenth century.

Right: The staircase in the front
entry appears to have been
magically transported from
Massachusetts or Maine.

Barn Inspired

Tanner Home,
Teton Valley, Idaho

ca. 2008

I really debated whether to include our dwelling in this book, for although it is a "home," it is not a house. You see, we live in a barn. I include it for this reason: there are those who enjoy Early American home styles but have never gone there because they feel they can only afford a "normal" house. The next few pages are for you. That is why this home—barn—whatever—is included.

If you've read about John and Geri Stukel's home in this book, you are halfway through our story. In an effort to have a smaller mortgage and allow Johnna to be a stay-at-home mom, we sold our nineteenth-century hewn-log home to the Stukel family and began to build again next door, creating a little ten-acre historical farm. We called our good friend Denny Walker in Tallmadge, Ohio, picked an awesome mid-1800s timber-framed barn, and shipped it to Idaho, as the beginnings of our house. In the meantime we began construction of my

Johnna and I never tire of being surrounded by antiques. They comfort like an old friend.

We tried to re-create an ideal Early American barn look. studio, adding a kitchen so that it could be temporary living quarters during construction of the house. Since an old historical farmstead would have a house, a barn, and several outbuildings, we built the studio to look like a barn.

Enter a stumbling economy. None of us have complete control over the world around us. Therefore we sometimes have to develop a Plan B. Just as we were about to start on the house we could see the writing on the wall, and subsequently opted to hold off on its construction. Quite honestly, we felt the studio barn would be large enough to meet our needs for a long time. It was built using salvaged materials that I had collected over several years. I walked through the stacks of old lumber, listing what I had, and designed the building according to that inventory. Our mantra became, "Don't buy anything that you can scrounge!" Though the wiring, insulation, framing lumber, and roofing are new, almost all else is reclaimed. The moral to the story is that Early American style can be done on a budget, if necessary. One could follow similar practices with a home—eschewing the "barn look." An added bonus for us is that the research for this book has given us countless new ideas when we are finally able to build the house!

Our Early American barn–influenced kitchen, with painted, rough-sawn walls. The antique farmhouse sink was given to us. Notice the flea market light fixture and old galvanized-tin kitchen countertop.

What began as my painting studio ended up as our
master bedroom. On a whim I created this window
seat with leftover barn timbers.

The painting studio turned master bedroom. It would have made an awesome studio—but makes a decent bedroom!

When Guests
Come *to* Visit

CABINS

We live near Jackson Hole, Wyoming. Around here there is a common saying: "We get nine months of winter and three months of company!" Some people love to have visitors, while others almost detest it. I suppose there is no right or wrong—just contrasting points of view. I saw a sign recently that read "Welcome friends!—Relatives by appointment only!" Many of the homes that we visited had guest accommodations of one type or another. Most had a guest bedroom or two, and many of the homeowners related that they love to have visitors—especially those with grandchildren. Several of the homes also had separate outbuildings that served as guest quarters. These were often as

Another use for outbuildings and guest quarters: they make a great place to store our collections—all of the stuff that won't fit in the house anymore! As an artist and writer, it is my duty to acquire lots of things to look at while I'm contemplating my next project.

well thought out, as well decorated, and as quaint as the homes themselves. I include some of them here for your enjoyment.

I'll never forget a vacation that Johnna and I took to Lancaster County, Pennsylvania. We stayed at an old farmhouse, surrounded by beautiful countryside and Early American farm buildings. Inside the primitive but cozy guest rooms, antique furnishings, quilts, and other objects

This old hewn-log cabin nestles into the woods of Virginia's Blue Ridge Mountains. It belongs to Jack and Cri Marshall.

decorated the entire room. The most memorable part of our visit occurred when, over a delicious country breakfast and friendly conversation, we were interrupted every few minutes by the clip-clop of horses on the street, for there happened to be an Amish auction that morning about a half mile down the road. One of the joys of being surrounded by old country ways, whether permanently in a home or temporarily at a lodging place, is that we get to transport ourselves to a simpler time, a simpler place, away from life's hustle and bustle.

My point, therefore, is simply this: if you create a special ambiance in your guest area, whether that area be a room or a separate building, your guests are bound to have a special experience. If you allow them to escape their stressful life for just a few short hours or days, they will feel a comfort that all of us crave, and visiting you will become even more of a treat. I'll let you decide whether that is a desirable thing or not.

David T. and Lora Smith's guesthouse is packed with more antiques and reproduction pieces from the Workshops of David T. Smith, similar to their cottage. Everywhere are treats for the eyes.

Above: My little studio cabin. To get to it, one simply hops into one's time machine and sets the dial to "a more peaceful era." Soon one finds oneself at the cabin.

Left: Inside the antique Marshall cabin getaway. Their main residence is nearby.

In the name of "roughing it," Jack and Cri Marshall's cabin has no modern conveniences. Water is carried by hand from a spring a short distance from the cabin, and the privy stands in the opposite direction down another path.

We visited David T. and Lora Smith on a cool autumn day, so David had the old cookstove burning and insisted on baking a batch of cookies in it. I, of course, had to accommodate by eating several—just to be a gracious guest, you understand.

Country Images

I hope you have enjoyed reading and viewing this book as much as I have enjoyed putting it together. I'm sure you can tell that I am fascinated with Early American styles of architecture and home design, as are the other homeowners in this book. Nothing says "home" to me the way that Early American style does. It allows us to escape from the modern, stressful world. It lets us bask in the warmth and friendship of family. It gives us appreciation for those who have gone before us—pioneers, settlers, farmers, gristmill owners—the list is endless. Early American style connects us with our ancestors in tangible ways. It will never go out of style or look dated; it went through the "dated" stage years ago and reemerged timeless and stylish. It will never go out of style because so much of it is based on classic design principles— principles that have been proven for thousands of years to be appealing to the human eye. It smells of apple pie baked in a wood cookstove, and sounds like a crackling fire in the hearth. It is simple, warm, cozy, and quaint—everything that home should be.

Along this journey, Johnna, photographer Brian Brown, and I have taken thousands of photographs, which have been condensed down to a hundred and some for this book. Many of the photos were not of houses, but of people, such as the kind Amish folk in Indiana and Iowa, historic sites, and the beautiful countryside. I couldn't visit New England without a stop at Old Sturbridge Village, and the restored historic sites of the LDS Church in the eastern United States are always an inspiration. I love old farms and fields and the rural countryside. These

types of images abound throughout our nation—we are blessed to live where we do. So, in closing, I offer some of the images that weren't necessarily of Early American homes, but of the American countryside— images that evoke a feeling of Early American style that I thought you might enjoy seeing.

Early American style is marked by peaceful, simple scenes—so refreshing compared to today's hectic world.

Photograph at bottom right taken at Old Sturbridge Village, Sturbridge, MA.

If one listens closely, historic settings, edifices, and objects seem to tell stories—
refreshingly new while comfortably familiar.

Photograph at top left taken at Old Sturbridge Village, Sturbridge, MA.

Textures play an important part in old country settings—weathered barnwood, stone and brick, a farmer's straw hat, even the feathers and fur of farm animals.

Photographs at center left and right taken at Old Sturbridge Village, Sturbridge, MA.

Late eighteenth– and early nineteenth–century buildings and objects are characterized by clean, plain lines—sparse in embellishments, abundant in the simplicity of common sense.

Early American style seems a bit incomplete without the added personality of a few scattered outbuildings and farm animals.

There are many historic farms—some official historic landmarks, some not—scattered throughout our nation's countryside, with visual treats and hundreds of ideas for those who wish to emulate Early American settings.

Photographs at top left and bottom taken at Old Sturbridge Village, Sturbridge, MA.

A covered bridge, a blacksmith's shop, and a simple dirt lane. While modern buildings and landscapes may be practical and refined, they often lack the charm of yesteryear.

Photographs at center left, bottom left, and right taken at Old Sturbridge Village, Sturbridge, MA.

So important, but usually subordinate in the American landscape, is the humble fence. It ties country edifices to their surroundings—a transitional design element between the man-made and the natural.

Photographs at top and bottom left taken at Old Sturbridge Village, Sturbridge, MA.

Early American style is unpretentious. "Grandiose" is never quite all it's cracked up to be—never as charming as a simple barnyard, root cellar, outbuilding, or even a spare, black Amish buggy.
Photograph at bottom left taken at Old Sturbridge Village, Sturbridge, MA.

Thank you for taking this journey with me—
and may God bless.